Ghost Layers

& Color Washes

Katie Pasquini Masopust

THREE STEPS TO SPECTACULAR QUILTS

C&T PUBLISHING

Dedication

To the man who makes

everything possible

all the time—

Bobby

Acknowledgments

Randi, for her invisible threads that hold me together

Sherry, for her nibs and nobs

Jody, for her big heart

All of my students who inspired me so much

Brad, who tolerates my absences

Don Gregg, for his perspective

Pfaff sewing machine company and their wonderful support group

---

Copyright © 2000 by Katie Pasquini Masopust

How-to photos and Ilustrations ©2000 by C&T Publishing

Development Editor: Cyndy Lyle Rymer
Technical Editor: Karyn Hoyt
Copy Editors: Randi Perkins and Steve Cook
Cover Design: Kris Yenche
Book Design: Nancy Koerner
Design Direction: Diane Pedersen
Graphic Illustrations: Aliza Kahn and Kirstie L. McCormick
Production Assistants: Kirstie L. McCormick and Stephanie Muir
Front Cover Image: *Passages—Pecos* by Katie Pasquini Masopust, 50" x 65", 1997.
Back Cover Image: *Fruit in a Bowl* by Katie Pasquini Masopust, 30" x 24", 2000
Photography: Quilts and how-to photos by Hawthorne Studio; location photos by Katie Pasquini Masopust, other quilt photos as noted.

Attention Teachers:

C&T Publishing, Inc. encourages you to use this book as a text for teaching. Contact us at 800-284-1114 or www.ctpub.com for more information about the C&T Teachers Program.

Library of Congress Cataloging-in-Publication Data

Pasquini Masopust, Katie.
    Ghost layers and color washes : three steps to spectacular quilts /
Katie Pasquini Masopust
        p.   cm.
    ISBN 1-57120-150-5
1. Quilting. 2. Color in textile crafts. I. Title.
TT835.P3665 2001
746.46--dc21

                                        00-011043

Published by C&T Publishing, Inc.
P.O. Box 1456
Lafayette, California 94549

Printed in Hong Kong

10   9   8   7   6   5   4   3   2   1

Contents

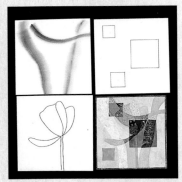

Eva Jalkotzy-Henneberry

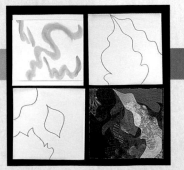

Patricia Ingersoll

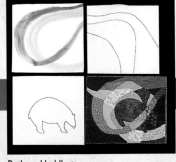

Barbara Huddleston

Katie

Introduction

I have been making quilts for over twenty years; my style has changed several times over this period. For the last six years, I have been very happy making my Fractured Landscape quilts. I thought this style would last me a lifetime, but I began to tire of my work and found myself less than excited when going into my studio. I needed a change.

I live in Santa Fe, where there is an unending supply of inspiration in the landscapes and the arts of New Mexico. I decided to take a walk up Canyon Road; it is a narrow street in the old style with traditional adobe buildings that are filled with art galleries. I entered each gallery to absorb the inspiration of others.

One of the galleries contained an oil painting that looked as if the canvas had been scraped to remove the first painting, with a second design painted over the top. There were parts of the original that seemed to float in and out of the top painting. It looked as if there were ghosts of the original painting hiding in the new layer. These transparent images gave me an idea.

I chose a photograph of an archway in an old adobe church. I took this photograph because of the light and shadow created by an unseen ladder at the end of the archway. I enlarged the shapes created by this play of light and shadow, and drew

Original photo of archway represented in Passages—Pecos

them on either side of the original archway. These shapes would be interpreted as lighter than the values from the original photograph. Excited by this, I drew bricks that mimicked the chevron of bricks at the end of the archway; these would be done in darker values than the background.

As I began to sort my fabrics to use for the values in the photograph, I realized if I followed the photograph I would only be using beige; I don't do beige quilts!

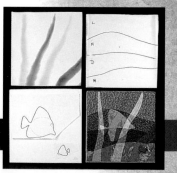

Deborah Bakke

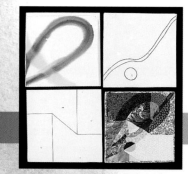

Judy Marble

Barbara McBride

I returned to my painting background and decided to do an abstract watercolor painting that I could superimpose over the first two layers to create a more colorful quilt.

Now this was electrifying—my piece actually had three layers: the original drawing from the photograph, the ghost or transparency of bricks and the ladders, and finally bright colors to liven the drab adobe colors!

I enjoy making these quilts and love teaching my students how to add more layers of visual interest to their quilts.

The first part of this book explains the three-step design process: creating a base layer on which to build, adding a ghost layer to create more depth and transparency, and making a painting to add color. The second half explains the process by showing my quilts and those of my students.

Enjoy and Create!

Passages—Pecos, 50" x 65," 1997. From the collection of Randi Perkins.

The Pecos is an area in northern New Mexico, just outside of Santa Fe, where the Pecos River and the Pecos National Monument are located. Several friends and I spent the day there, exploring the ruins and catching up on old times. My favorite ruin was an old adobe church. There was a wonderful archway that led from the outside courtyard to a passageway to the church.

I chose to enlarge the shapes created by the play of shadow and light, and placed them on either side of the archway as a lighter ghost. I also enlarged the chevron of bricks seen on the back wall of the arch and placed them throughout the quilt as darker ghosts. My painting was done with red, yellow, and blue; the white areas were interpreted as the original adobe colors.

Materials List

2" brush—an inexpensive brush used to make the paint strokes in the watercolor wash process

3" foam brush—to prep the watercolor paper

acetate—optional material for the creation of a larger quilt (see the section entitled *The Masterpiece*, page 34)

ball-point pen—for drawing the pattern onto the stabilizer

batting—I use Hobbs™ wool batting

colored pencils—for coloring in the pattern

compass—for making ghost circles

darning foot—for free-motion stitching

fabric—lots of it, in all values and fiber contents

glue stick—to attach fabric to stabilizer when necessary

iron—lightweight, with a good point at the end

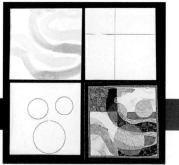

Jerry Paddock

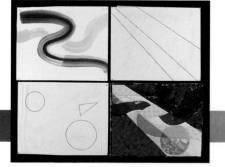

Carole Preddice

Cindy Turner

monofilament thread—to machine appliqué all pieces in place

palette—for paint mixing (can be cardboard plate)

pencils—a number 2 pencil for drawing and fabric pencils for marking the fabric

pigma pen—for drawing on acetate for masterpiece quilts

6-ply railroad board—a lightweight cardboard for templates

ruler—for drawing straight lines

sewing machine—with a zigzag stitch

spray adhesive—for mounting the pattern onto the railroad board, and for basting

spray starch—for turning fabric edges over cardboard

Sulky Totally Stable® stabilizer—for attaching all of the fabric pieces before appliquéing in place

stiletto—for turning edges without burning your fingers

threads—in a rainbow assortment

tracing paper—at least 18" square for drawing

watercolor paints—in primary colors for the color wash process

watercolor paper—for the color wash

Throughout this book are studies that show the process. The color wash is always shown in the upper left, the base layer is in the upper right, the ghost is in the lower left, and the quilt in the lower right.

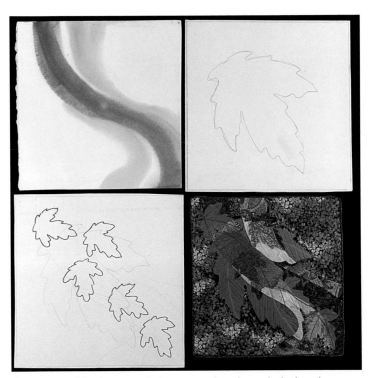

An overview of the three-part design process: the color wash, the base layer, the ghost layer, a block by Katie.

Beverly Fine

Cynthia Buchanan

Katie

The Base

When working on my pieces, I usually start with a photograph as my base. I do a line drawing on acetate from the photograph. These pieces can become very complicated; so, in order to teach the process, we will start with an 18" square of tracing paper instead of a photograph.

Begin by drawing a simple block. I have learned that "simple" means different things to every person. What seems simple as a single 18" block becomes complicated when the other two layers (ghost and painting) are added. Let's define "simple" as a block consisting of four units. These can be made with straight or curved lines, as long as there are only four units.

Here are some examples.

Sample Base Blocks

Virginia Freal

Katie

Jo-Ann Golenia

More Sample Base Blocks

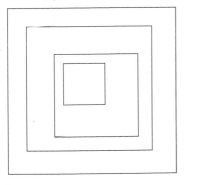 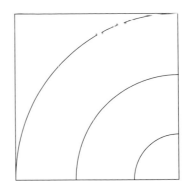 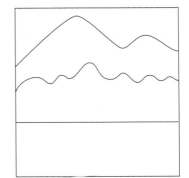

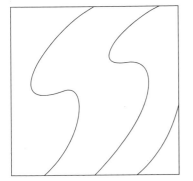  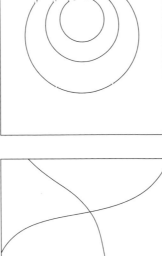

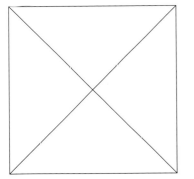 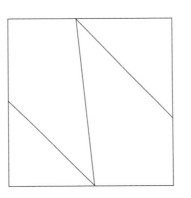 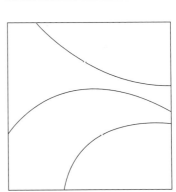

In the examples throughout, the base layer is always shown in the upper right square.

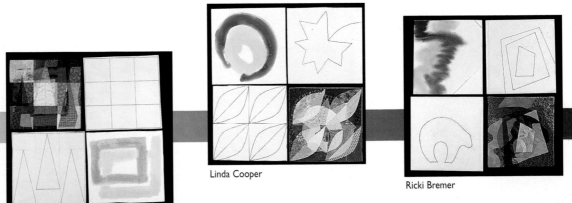

Joan Clemons

Linda Cooper

Ricki Bremer

Adding the Ghost Layer

The ghost layer adds depth and richness to the piece. Objects float in and out of focus on the base like a ghost. They can compliment the base design by having elements in common, or they can contrast, using totally different shapes. The "ghosts" add interest and mystery.

The ghost is a shape that will be lighter or darker than the base block colors. These shapes should be simple, at least to start with. Three shapes are enough for a first project (circles, squares, triangles, or organic shapes with curved lines, such as birds or fishes), and they should not overlap each other. Draw these shapes freehand or with a ruler and compass on a piece of tracing paper. If you are uncertain of placement, cut these shapes out of paper, then move them around on top of the tracing paper until the placement is pleasing. As the final step, copy them onto the tracing paper.

Here are some examples.

Sample Ghost Shapes

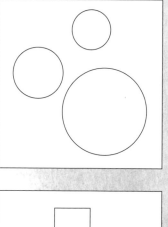

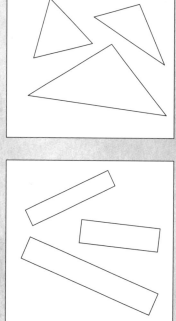

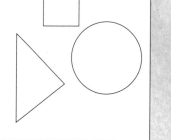

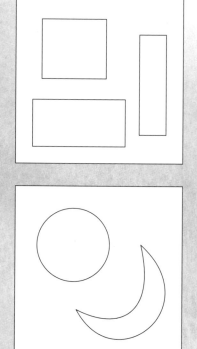

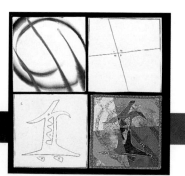

Dawn Crocetti

Grace Crocker

Judy Liebo

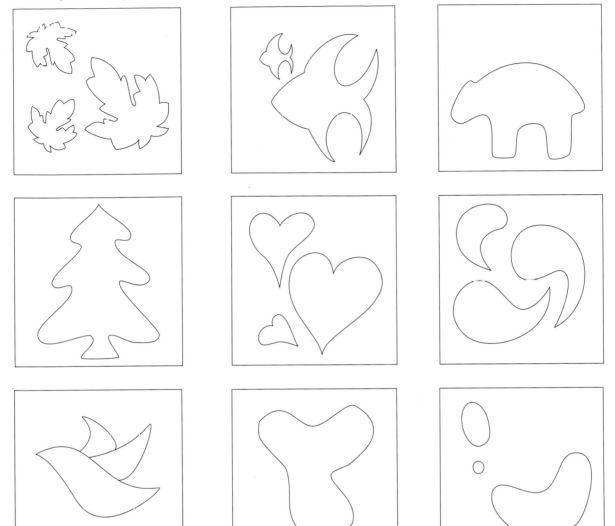

In the examples throughout, the ghost layer is the bottom left square.

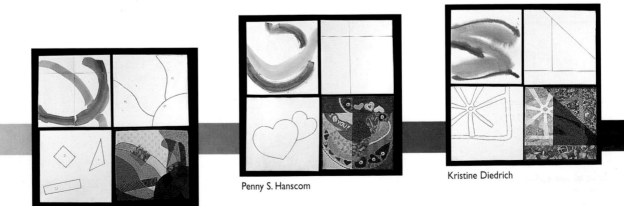

Karen L. Krause

Penny S. Hanscom

Kristine Diedrich

Creating a Color Wash

The purpose of the watercolor painting is to add color to enhance the line drawing. This allows you to use more colors in the quilt and adds a sense of play.

Make an abstract painting on good quality water-color paper. Use a 3" foam brush to evenly dampen an 18" (or larger) piece of watercolor paper. Place a good dollop of paint on a palette, add enough water to completely saturate a 2" brush. Now stand back and make a large swipe of paint. Doesn't it feel good to be painting? Use a second color of paint and make a second swipe. Remember to keep it simple; you will see why soon.

Here are some examples.

Color Wash Samples

Babs Robinson

Emma Allebes

Katie

More Color Wash Samples

In the examples throughout, the paintings are shown in the upper left corner.

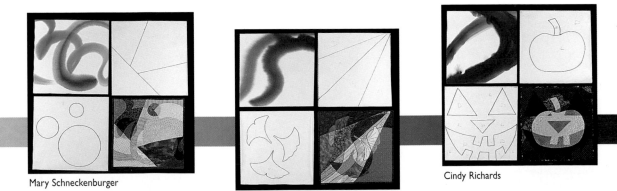

Mary Schneckenburger

Missie Carpenter

Cindy Richards

Combining the Layers

Now comes the fascinating part—combining all of the layers. Each of the three layers you've created at this point is not very interesting by itself, but wait and see what happens when you put all three together.

If you are unsure about creating a design of your own, you can use the samples from the previous sections to put together a combination. Use tracing paper to copy your chosen blocks, then have these enlarged on a photocopy machine to the 18" size.

Combined Layers   Base   Ghost

1. Layer the base and ghost together to see what happens.

2. With a third piece of tracing paper, trace both of the original layers together—the ghost and base—as one.

Patricia F. Heydt

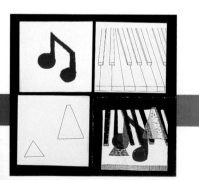

Maureen Hendricks

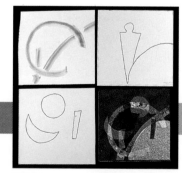

Judy Sauer

3. Lay this third piece of tracing paper with the base and the ghost shapes over the painting, moving it around until you are satisfied with the placement of the paint strokes. Trace the edges of the paint strokes. This is the pattern.

Combined Layers

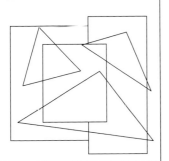

Colorwash

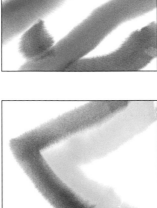

Pattern

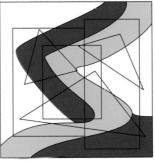

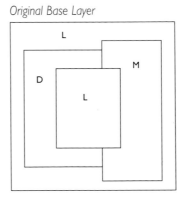

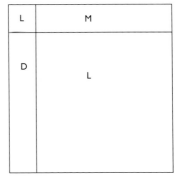

4. Return to the original base layer and label the value of each of the four units on the base layer. This labeling is arbitrary. The values you use are:

L (Light)   M (Medium)   D (Dark)

Original Base Layer

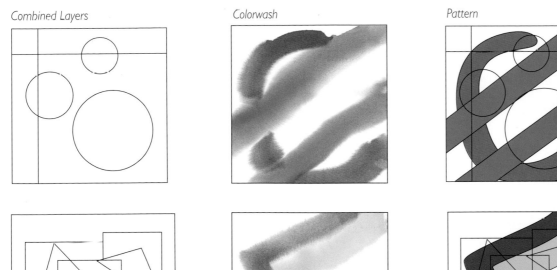

5. Return to the original ghost layer and label the ghost layer with either L or D. This means that your ghost will be lighter or darker than the base block (don't use M at this point; the ghost can't be more "medium" than the base layer).

Original Ghost Layer

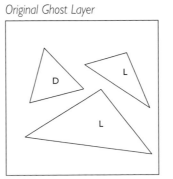

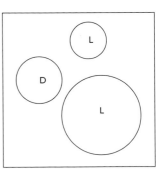

Original Base Layer

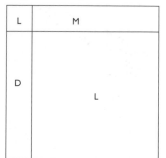

Pattern

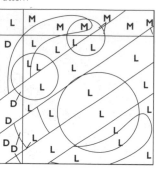

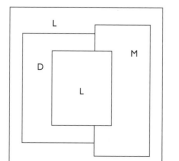

Original Ghost Layer

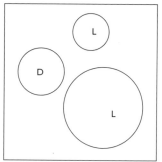

Pattern

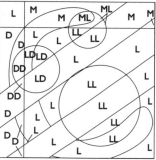

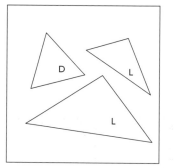

6. Return to the pattern. Refer to the original base layer and label all of the new shapes in the base units in your combination as L, M, or D. Each of the base shapes should have one value letter.

Labeling the pattern.

Refer back to the ghost drawing and give the new shapes in the ghost a value letter. Each of the ghost shapes should have two letters: one for the base that it is on and one for the value of the ghost.

Pattern

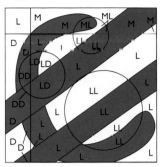

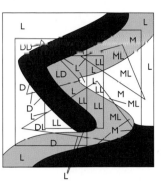

7. With colored pencils, fill in the color of the brush strokes very lightly.

Using a spray adhesive, spray mount your pattern onto 6-ply poster board; this is your pattern that is cut apart into templates.

8. Trace the pattern, without labels, on another piece of tracing paper. Pin this "map" to your design wall.

9. Trace another copy (no labels) onto an 18" square of Sulky Totally Stable using a ballpoint pen; this will be the foundation used to place and stitch all of the fabric pieces. Trim the excess.

Any of the illustrations from the previous pages can be enlarged and used for your beginning project.

You are now ready to sort your fabrics.

Map and stabilizer copy.

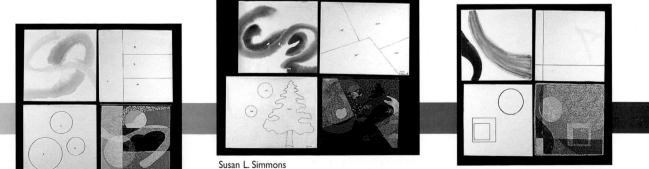

Margie Rudolph

Susan L. Simmons

Sheila Bayley

Color and Fabric Sorting

I have sorted my fabrics into seven steps for years (introduced in *Fractured Landscapes* as "Katie's Seven Step Program"), and it made my color choices so much easier for Fractured Landscape quilts. When I began to create ghost layer quilts, I quickly realized that the seven steps work great for this process, too.

1. First, sort your fabrics by color.

2. Sort each color into values from light to dark in seven separate steps.

    • The first pile includes very pale shades of a color (white also goes in this step).

    • The seventh stack of fabrics includes very dark shades of a color, including blacks.

    • The five steps in between include a range from light to dark.

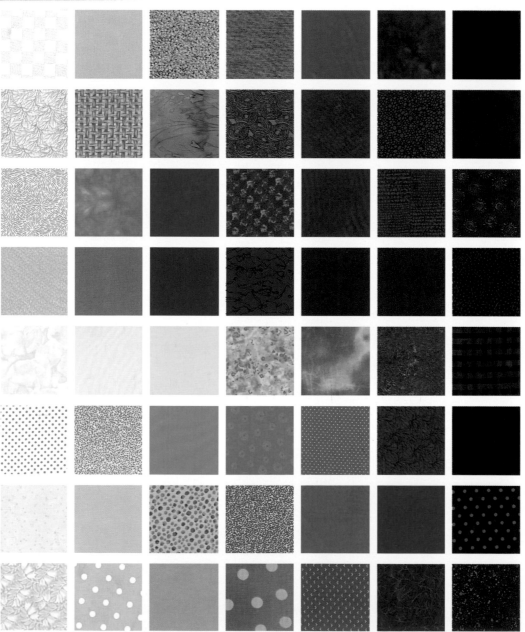

Fabrics sorted into value families

3. Place your fabrics with the folded edges up in a drawer or box, or facing you on a table. Stand back and fine tune until you see distinct value differences in all of the steps. This may seem difficult, but once you get them laid out you will find that everything else is easier.

Most people like to buy bright-colored fabrics, so their steps 3, 4, and 5 are very full, while the paler shades in steps 1 and 2 and the darkest shades in steps 6 and 7 have fewer pieces. I force myself to seek out the pale tints because they give light to the quilt. I love to find really good number sevens—they add depth to any quilt.

These will be the seven steps you will draw from when choosing your fabrics.

You will need three hues sorted into the seven steps: the two colors that match your paint strokes and a third color to represent the unpainted areas.

Follow this chart to assign each of the letters on a template a number.

1	2	3	4	5	6	7
	L		M		D	

These numbers will correspond to the seven value piles of fabrics. When there is just one letter for a base piece, it will receive a 2 for Light, a 4 for Medium, or a 6 for Dark. When numbering the ghosts, go to the number of the first letter—the base—then, if the second letter (the ghost) is L, move one step to the left; if the second letter is D, move one step to the right.

The number on the template will tell you which value to choose; the color of the template (color for the paint strokes or white for the third color) will tell you the color to use.

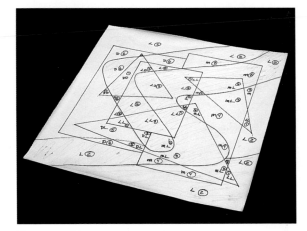

The map will keep you organized.

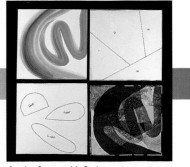

Sandra Stewart McCaslin

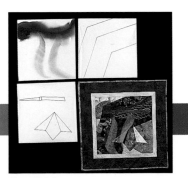

Katie Melich

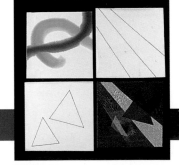

Kristi Leduc

Cutting and Turning the Edges

Cut each template from the railroad board, then choose an appropriate fabric (indicated by the color of the template and the value number).

Turn the fabric and the template wrong side up and draw around the edge of the template; cut the fabric at least $^1/4$" larger all around than the template. It is not necessary to measure this accurately, just cut it visually $^1/4$" larger.

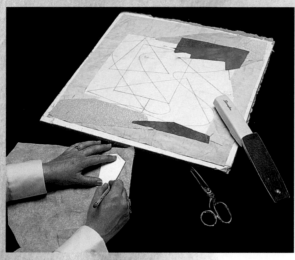

Trace around each template.

Place the template under the cut fabric on the map and staple or pin both in place.

Staple each piece on the map.

Cut all the pieces and place them on the map to see how it looks before you start to turn or sew anything.

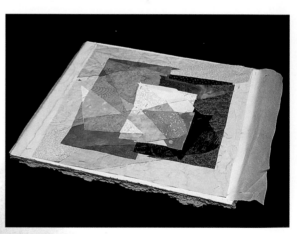

All pieces placed on the map.

Katie

Catherine Clay

Cassy LaVigne

Once all the pieces are cut and you are satisfied with your fabric choices, you need to attach all the pieces to the stabilizer copy.

There are a few different ways to construct these blocks: using raw-edge appliqué, fusing each piece to a base fabric instead of the stabilizer with a product such as Wonder Under®, or turning all the exposed edges as in traditional appliqué. I prefer to turn all of the exposed edges, because it gives strength to the quilt.

Take a piece and spray the wrong side of the fabric with spray starch. Lay the template upside down in place on the wrong side of the fabric piece. Clip any tight curves. Using a sewer's stiletto (to prevent burned fingers), turn the seam allowance over the cardboard of any edge that will be exposed, pressing with the iron until you have a sharp crease.

Press the seam allowance around the template.

Before you turn the edges on all of the pieces, check to see which actual edge will be on top or exposed—this will be the edge you need to turn. (Do not turn all of the edges, just the edges on the top. The other pieces will lie under the turned edges.)

Remove the template and lay the fabric in place on the stabilizer. Heat set it with the iron. Be sure to line up the turned edge of the fabric piece with the drawn line on the stabilizer so everything matches. Touch the tip of the iron to the piece to secure it. Slip the unturned edge of the next piece under this turned edge.

Heat setting the pieces on the stabilizer.

Continue until all the pieces are in place. Turn the block over and lightly press the stabilizer from the back to secure all the pieces. If there are places where the fabric does not touch the stabilizer, use a glue stick to tack it in place.

Now you are ready to sew.

Sewing

Pieces sewn to the stabilizer with a zigzag stitch.

All the pieces need to be sewn to the stabilizer. I set my machine to zigzag with a #2 width.

A darning foot or Big Foot™ is essential for free-motion work. Unlike a lot of quilters, I leave the feed dogs up when I free-motion because the friction created helps move the fabric along.

Use your darning foot with the feed dogs up to free-motion stitch around all the edges. The "points" of the zigzag stitch should fall on either side of the fold line. It's a good idea to practice your stitching on a scrap piece of fabric first. You are in charge of how long the stitch is, even with

the feed dogs up, so you need to push the fabric through fairly fast or go really slow with your foot. Try to keep your stitches from falling too close together, or they will lose their "hidden" aspect. This technique will become easier once you practice. Leaving the feed dogs up helps you develop a rhythm. You can also go backwards when necessary.

I find this zigzag method to be even more invisible than the blind hem stitch, and it is easier and faster. Use a neutral thread in the bobbin (gun-metal gray for the dark and medium sections and a soft gray on the light section) and a monofilament thread in the top.

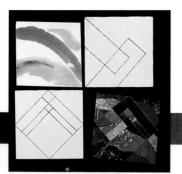

Ann Ferkovich

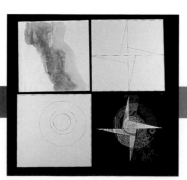

Ricki Smith Selva

Aurelle S. Locke

Once everything is stitched in place, tear off the stabilizer using the "fatty thigh method": Lay the project upside down on your thigh and dig into the soft surface with your nail to rip the stabilizer and tear off the majority of it. If you do not remove the stabilizer, it will be harder to quilt, and very stiff when finished.

Cut a backing fabric and a batting at least an inch bigger all around than the block. Lay backing, batting, and top, in that order, on a table. Instead of basting with needle and thread or pins, I prefer to use a spray basting adhesive. Just be sure you spray in a well-ventilated area. Fold the top halfway back and lightly spray the batting. Smooth the first half of the top in place on the batting, then do the same for the other half. Turn the piece over and repeat for the backing.

Removing the stabilizer.

Press from the back to flatten the layers. Now you can begin to machine quilt.

Keep in mind that using the spray adhesive works well for smaller pieces. A larger quilt will require regular basting because it is handled more and the spray adhesive loses its binding abilities.

Baste the layers together with spray adhesive.

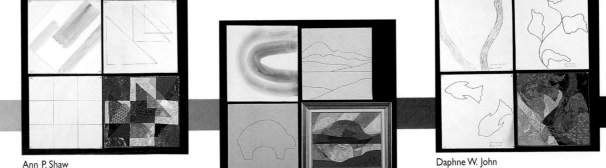

Ann P. Shaw

Martha Perrins-Dallman

Daphne W. John

Machine Quilting

All kinds of threads can be used to machine quilt. I find threads with longer fibers work the best as they do not break as easily as shorter-fiber threads; Mölnlycke®, Mettler, and Gutermann® threads are in the long fiber category. I prefer to use Gutermann thread; I like their color choices and they seem to hold up better.

A darning foot or Big Foot™ is essential for free-motion quilting. As mentioned in the previous chapter, I leave the feed dogs up when I free-motion quilt.

Use the same color thread in both the bobbin and the top; this adds a wonderful texture and interest to the back of the quilt. It also prevents the bobbin thread from accidentally showing up on the top.

Set your machine to the zigzag stitch and the stitch width to 0. This combination will create a straight stitch that will go smoothly into a satin stitch while stitching. Use the satin stitch to create texture, to add accents where the color choices don't show enough contrast, and to cover any mistakes or holes you might have.

Place your piece under the darning foot with the feed dogs still up. Be sure to bring the bobbin thread up to the top before you start to sew—this will eliminate the need to trim the threads from the back when you are finished. Then just play. Try following the print of the fabric or creating texture with the many stitching possibilities shown here. Or make up your own patterns by "doodling" with the needle. For a good satin stitch, gradually increase the stitch width as you sew. Press down hard on the foot pedal to sew fast, but move the fabric slowly in order to get the stitches to line up one right after the other. Be patient. Learn your rhythm and your machine's.

Tension causes problems for many people. I find that many different factors can make your tension go crazy. Rather than deal with a definite setting, I play with the upper tension until the stitch looks good. But what often happens is when I next sit down to sew, using the same setting, the tension is not right. I am of the school of "Just Play With It Until It Is Right." That might not sound very helpful, but it works for me.

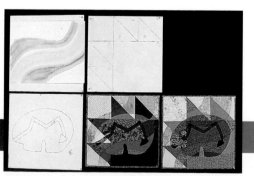

Patricia F. Heydt

Babs Robinson

Jenny D. Patrick

Samples of Free-Motion Quilting

1A Little Circles	3C Waves
2A Big Circles	4C Weave
3A Maze	1D Water
4A Twigs	2D Branches and Twigs
1B Squares	3D Undulating satin stitch
2B stipple with crossing	4D Thick and thin satin stitch
3B stipple without crossing*	1E Freeform
4B Echo	2E Computer
1C Leaves	3E Bricks
2C Stars	4E Swirls

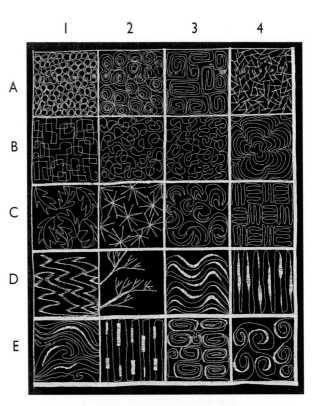

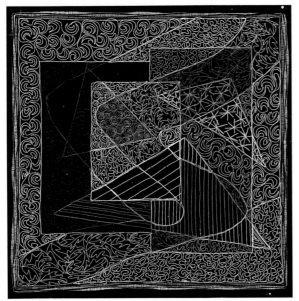

Machine quilting sample

*(The "rule" for stippling has always been never to cross over the stitching line; I prefer to think that crossing over in a section once or twice is a "mistake," but crossing ten or twelve times is a pattern.)

Judy Taubinger

Anita McSorley

Sharon Little

Satin Stitch Quilting Using a Regular Foot

An alternate method to create a straight satin stitch is to use the regular foot and set the length very close to create a solid satin stitch. For example, take a look at the mortar in *Little Getty* and other Getty Museum quilts on pages 47 and 49. Use this when a very straight line is needed.

Scribble Technique

Place the quilt sandwich under the needle, and with a straight stitch "scribble" the design. This technique was used to create the bricks in *Doorways*, page 42.

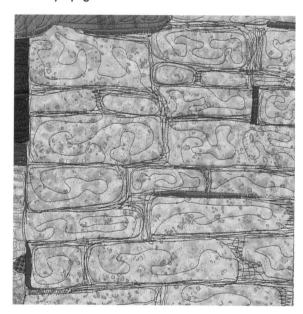

Binding

Bind and be proud. I use a 1 1/2"-wide bias strip folded in half for a tight, thin binding. Sew the raw edge to the front, trim the raw edge, and roll to the back and hand stitch.

Most people say that once they have done one study from start to finish, a second piece is much simpler. I would suggest doing a second study before starting your masterpiece.

Binding added.

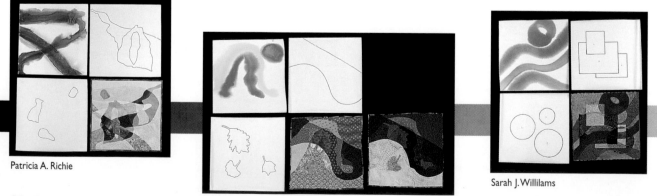

Patricia A. Richie

Joann Mellon

Sarah J. Willilams

Fruit in a Bowl Project

This pattern is called Fruit in a Bowl. It can be adapted in any way you choose. The following instructions will be a review of "The Process" chapters.

Fruit in a Bowl, 30" x 24", 2000.

1. Take this pattern to a copy shop that has a machine that can enlarge up to 36", and have the pattern enlarged to your desired size. This quilt was enlarged 495% to a size of 30" × 24". Have two copies made.

2. Trace the enlarged pattern onto the stabilizer. I use a blue pen to trace the base lines, a black pen to trace the ghosts, and a purple or other color pen to trace the paint lines. Pin one copy to your design wall and mount the other copy to the railroad board with the spray adhesive.

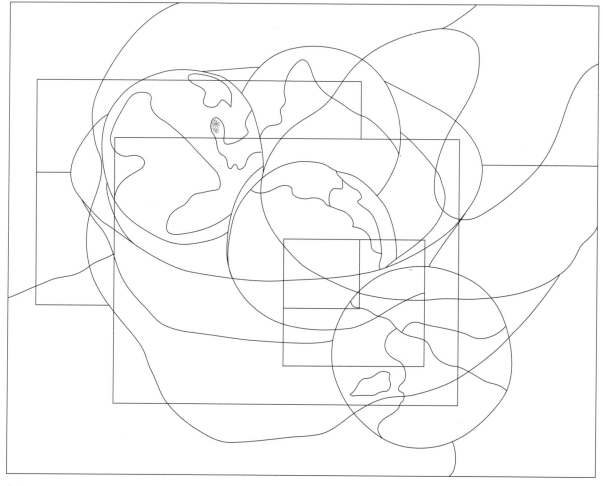

Project map.

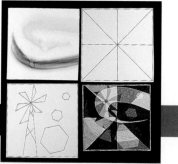

Jeane Ives

Diane Harris

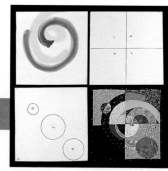

Carol Golden

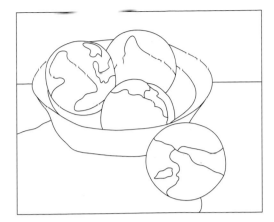

Base layer.

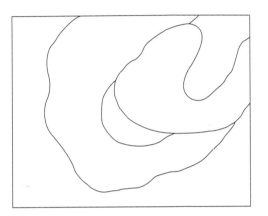

Color wash.

3. Decide on the colors and values you would like to use; the paint and background colors can be changed in any way you wish. On the railroad board copy, color in the paint lines and label as on pages 15 and 16.

4. Following the instructions on pages 18–21, cut out the fabrics and pin or staple them to the stabilizer on the wall. When you are happy with your choices, begin to turn the edges and apply them to the stabilizer.

5. Stitch around the edge of each piece with an invisible zigzag free-motion stitch.

6. Tear off the stabilizer and spray baste the top and backing to the batting.

7. Quilt the piece using a free-motion straight stitch and add texture and definition with a free-motion zigzag.

8. Square up the quilt, add a binding, and be proud.

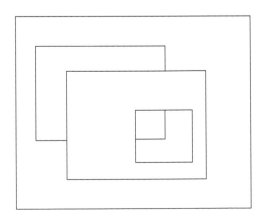

Ghost layer.

Creating a Masterpiece

The masterpiece is done much like the studies. Instead of a simple base layer, I make a more complicated drawing from a photograph or from my imagination. I draw the shapes of the images and the values within. I then choose a ghost that is either an object in the photograph or one that is in total opposition to the photograph. Next I do a colorwash or "painting," for which there are three possibilities:

1. A watercolor painting that disregards the "color" of the photograph.

2. A "mind painting" in which I decide on the colors in my mind and do not do an actual painting.

3. The photo itself. When I like the color of the photograph, I don't need to do an actual painting—the colors of the photo are enough.

Choose a photograph with good composition and a variety of shapes and sizes. I enlarge the negative to a high-quality 11" x 18" or larger print. Sometimes I combine several photographs to get a good composition, as in the *Antelope Canyon* and *Painted Canyon* quilts.

Sometimes you have to play with photo arrangements for good composition.

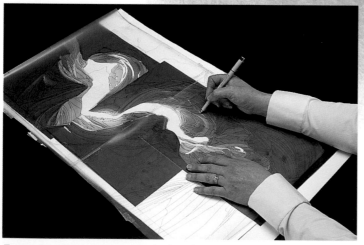

Tracing the photograph to create the base layer.

Place a piece of frosted acetate, matte side up, over the photograph and draw the image with a Pigma .01 black pen. Draw around the shapes of the objects and around the value changes within the objects. This becomes the base layer.

On a tracing paper overlay, play with different ghosts that will float in and out of the base layer. The ghosts can be either an object in the base that is enlarged and superimposed on top, or abstract shapes that create more interest, such as squares or circles that interplay with the base.

If a painting is required, cut several pieces of watercolor paper the size of the photo, wet them down, and paint them with quick, flowing strokes.

After the paintings have dried, lay them under the acetate drawing to see which one looks best. Add the lines of the paint strokes to the acetate.

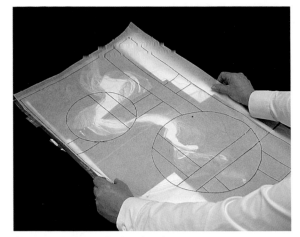

Playing with shapes for the ghost layer.

Take the acetate drawing to a copy center or blueprint shop to be enlarged to the full size of your quilt design. Get three copies made: one is spray-basted to the template material for the pattern, the second is

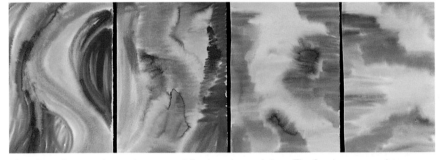

A variety of watercolor washes created for the color wash layer. The fourth one was chosen.

pinned or stapled to the pin-up wall for your map, the third copy is used to trace the pattern to the stabilizer. I refer to the actual photograph for the values. I cut out my pieces and staple them to the "map" on my pin-up wall. When I am satisfied with my choices, I attach them to the stabilizer as for the previous examples, stitch all in place, and quilt.

The pages that follow explore the thought processes involved with each masterpiece quilt. Searching out locations for my photographs is half of the fun, and I share my adventures.

The first two quilts were transition pieces from Fractured Landscapes to Ghost Layers. In my work there are always several pieces that are a blend of the change in styles—there is not a definite break between styles. In *The Canyon* and *Grapes* the fracture lines can be seen as ghosts.

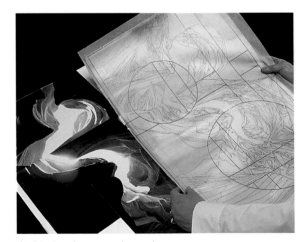

Auditioning the watercolor washes.

The Canyon

The Canyon, 86" x 54", 1995. Private collection.

Canyon De Chelly is in north central Arizona in the Navajo Nation. After hearing about this wonderful place, I made a reservation to take a guided tour of the canyon. My husband and my friend Sherry went with me. We arrived late one November day after a seven-hour drive from Santa Fe. In anticipation of our tour, we drove around the top edge of the canyon, peering at the wonders that lay below. This heightened our excitement about the day to follow. We had a great guide who had lived in the bottom of the canyon as a child. He knew all of the stories and myths that mothers told their children about the incredible rock formations.

Drawing for The Canyon: *The trees were added for visual interest.*

We spent a wonderful day driving through the canyon, and were in awe of marvelous rocks, mountains, rivers, ruins, and cave paintings.

The Canyon, which was inspired by that incredible trip, was a commission piece. The buyer chose a photo of the wall of the canyon, but did not want any blue in the sky. We eventually settled on the colors of a photo he provided of a yellow Missouri sky at sunset. This was one of the last fractured landscapes I did, and it seems to cross over into the Ghost Layers realm. The piece was fractured with squares within squares, on and on to the center, where there is a very light square set on point. The ghosts are the squares and the colors are true, so there was no painting.

The River

The River, 45" x 60", 1995. Private collection.

The same people who own *The Canyon* commissioned this quilt. It was done from a photograph of a river in France. The Ghost/Fracture lines are rectangles. I added more colors to the drab photograph.

I recommend that everyone take a photography class. Photographs give you plenty of ideas for quilts and help you understand composition and light. You will see your surroundings in a new way, and get a different angle from the way everyone else looks at the same thing. After taking a photography class I feel that my work has improved.

Water Lilies

Water Lilies, 60" x 54", 1997. Collection of Suzy Sachs.

This quilt was inspired by a photograph I took while teaching in New Zealand. The ghost/fracture lines are rectangles, and the color is graduated from light in one corner to dark in the opposite corner in each of the rectangles. It reminds me of Monet's "Water Lilies."

Grapes

These photos were taken on the front porch of my friend Randi Perkin's house in northern California, where the most incredible grapes hung from the awning, shading us from the hot summer sun. I lay down on the deck and took several rolls of film. The fracture lines that represent grapes work well as a transparency. I did a "mind painting" and changed the colors of the grapes within each of the circles in *Grapes*, on page 37.

I wanted to try adding ghosts of grapes and a swipe of red and yellow paint to add color to the green grapes in the original photo.

Small Grapes, 18" x 28", 1997. Collection of Terrie Hancock Mangat.

Grapes, 96" x 60", 1996. Collection of Maureen and John Hendricks.

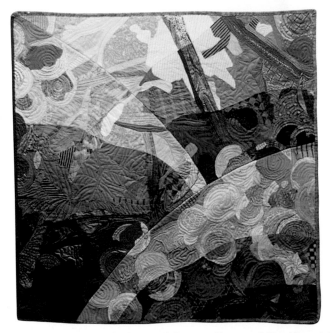

This was a small test for Grapes. Collection of Larry and Sheryl Pasquini.

Passion Flowers

Passion Flowers, 54" x 64," 1997. Collection of Kirk Turner.

I always have my camera with me because I never know when a wonderful picture will present itself. This one was especially surprising. I was pulling into a friend's driveway to pick her up for a meeting, and there in front of me was the most beautiful clematis. The light was just right (about an hour before sunset), intensifying the whiteness of the flowers and the depth of the shadows. I jumped out and took several pictures. The meeting was lost to me because I planned and made this quilt in my head that night.

I learned a lot from this piece. Two flower ghosts are hiding—and I mean *hiding*—in the center. One thing that doesn't work is having a ghost lighter than white! The ghost is lost where it overlaps the white flowers because the values are the same. Although, when the light streams in through the window, the shy flowers do glow! The painting was enclosed in the chevron-like sections, each one done in a different bright color.

Passages–Chaco Canyon

Passages—Chaco Canyon, 45" x 60," 1997. Collection of Maureen and John Hendricks.

One day I received a phone call from my friend Jody. She was very excited because she had just returned from a trip to Chaco Canyon, and she kept saying, "You have to go there with me; the whole time I was there I kept saying, 'Katie would make a quilt of this.'" I was game, so we chose a day and left at the crack of dawn (actually, dawn was a long way off). We wanted to get there when the light was best, which we found out later was about 11:30 am. Let's just say we did a lot of exploring before the light was right. I was totally blown away with this place!

Chaco Canyon is in central New Mexico; it is where the Anasazi Native Americans lived and built their dwellings. These dwellings were built in such a way that four or five doorways line up, one right behind the other. It is a photographer's heaven; I must have used about twelve rolls of film. The deep turquoise sky seen through the windows of orange rock was inspiring.

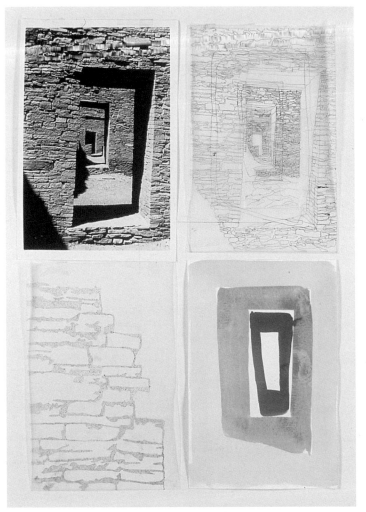

The ghost is a section of the bricks and mortar enlarged, and the painting is three rectangles of color that represent "doorways" through color and the "doorways" in my life. In the quilt, the rectangle of warm-color bricks is complementary to the color of the mortar. It was tricky to represent the depth in the photograph while following the colors of the very flat painting. I had to remember to be true to the values of the photograph.

Passages–Doorways

Passages—Doorways, 36" x 45", 1997. Collection of Maureen and John Hendricks.

After completing *Passages—Chaco Canyon,* with all of the zillions of teeny tiny bricks turned and stitched, I needed to do one with larger pieces!

I chose another photo of the Chaco doorways and reduced the large doorway, repeating it three times. The painting was a mind painting using bold saturated colors; all the detail was done with the quilting. The yellow is all one piece, with the bricks quilted using the scribble technique.

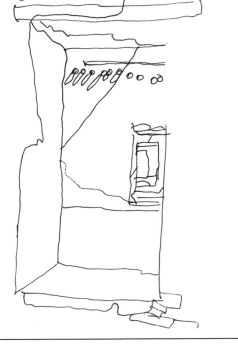

Rocks

At Chaco Canyon, you can actually hike up a steep trail to the rim and walk along it to look down at the ruins below. Jody and I are both afraid of heights; halfway up the trail we decided we should just see everything from ground level! There is a place below the rim where giant boulders have fallen. We walked through these huge rocks feeling like little elves; this picture is from inside the path that runs through the boulders.

I used a mind painting to create the bold colors, and a ghost layer of squares and stripes add interest to this piece. The ghost has nothing to do with the photograph, so it sets up a contradiction.

Rocks, 36" x 54", 1998.

The Getty Museum Quilts

One night I watched a report on television about the architect involved with the new J. Paul Getty Museum. The footage of the buildings had me under a spell. I was scheduled to teach at a conference in southern California just after the program aired, and decided to fly out early so I could visit the museum. When I called the museum, I was told it would be months before I could get a parking reservation in their garage, but I could park just down the hill at the Holiday Inn and take a shuttle up the hill. When calling for a reservation, don't be put off by the parking information; use the Holiday Inn! The museum was amazing! I photographed every inch of it. In fact, I took pictures for three hours before I even went inside to see the fabulous artwork. There are many buildings with wonderful details that make you feel like you are in a fairy tale.

This picture is one of the first I took; the closer I zoomed in, the better it looked.

I used a "mind painting" to make the structure bright in *Little Getty*. The ghost is made of clouds that should only be in the blue of the sky but also float over the concrete structure. This sets up a contrary image of the flowing clouds and the solid concrete.

Little Getty, 35" x 54", 1998.

The museum is made of two kinds of granite: one is very rough and one is completely smooth. These two textures would inspire any fiber artist. There is also a waterfall that starts as a tiny stream at the entrance and flows downhill, getting larger at each level. At the bottom, a huge waterfall drops into a pond with a floating maze, with gardens and walking paths all around. As you sit on a bench you can look up at the many buildings of the museum.

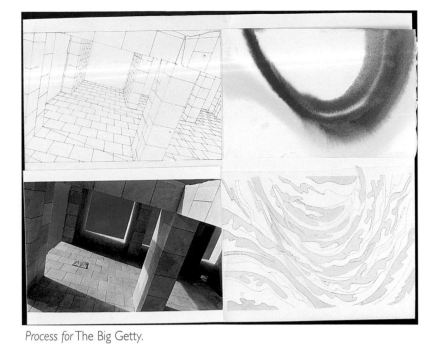

Process for The Big Getty.

After the success of *Little Getty* with its floating clouds and concrete, I made the *Big Getty*. I did the painting of the large curves first, then the ghost of clouds that follow the flow of the paint strokes. The mortar between the blocks was done with a satin stitch using the regular foot; I let the machine guide the fabric along. The more you look at this quilt, the more the concrete starts to flow and move. My friend calls this "vertigo on a flat plane."

The Big Getty, *81" x 54", 1998.*

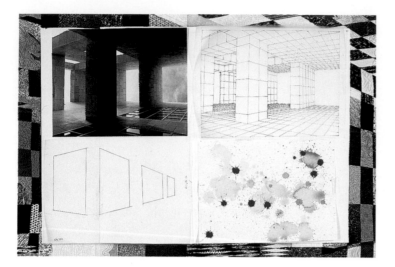

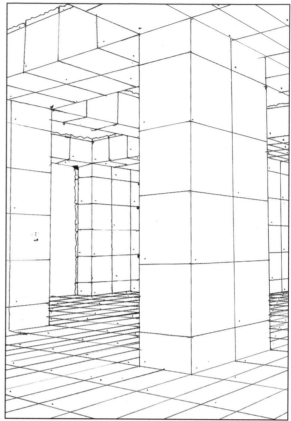

It took me three hours of photographing the out-side of the museum before I forced myself to go inside, but I am glad I did! Many years ago I took an art appreciation course in high school from my favorite teacher, Mr. Sullivan. Many of the paintings he used as examples of the masters were on the walls! Degas, Monet, Manet, Seurrat, Cezanne, and a Renoir that brought tears to my eyes. What an experience. . . .

The last in the Getty series features splots of paint. I stood on a chair with a brush loaded with paint and let it drop on the paper lying on the floor. The ghosts are four large rectangles in perspective that are interpreted as dark against the black and white prints.

Black and White Getty, 60" x 45", 1998. Collection of Maureen and John Hendricks.

The Canyon Quilts

I often see pictures of the slot canyons at many art and craft markets in New Mexico. They are incredible photographs, with the sun streaming down from above into deep, colorful canyons. They look like a magical place, not of this earth, and I never expected to ever find them, let alone go in and explore them.

For New Year's Eve, 1999, my husband, his son Brad, and I drove eight hours to Page, Arizona. I felt like we were on a wild goose chase; there was no way we would find what I had seen in the photos at the craft shows. We called the Page One Office Supply Store to see how we would find the canyons; they said that they would be taking tours in on New Year's Day! My dream was becoming attainable. We spent New Year's Eve in a dingy little hotel (only two were open; Page and Lake Powell are summer tourist towns).

Slot Canyon, on page 52, is the first in this series. I used a mind painting to add color and two circular ghosts, one lighter and the other darker, than the background.

Nature at its most abstract and beautiful.

Slot Canyon, 34" x 50", 1999.

The next day we met our tour guide and went into the Upper Antelope Canyon, a three-quarter-mile hike on a level sand bed. We were told to be very respectful of the canyons. The entrance is very plain and unassuming; again, I was sure this was not what I was looking for. Once out of the light and around the first bend, I lost my breath; it was one of the most natural, spiritual, beautiful places on earth. Even my husband and Brad were in awe!

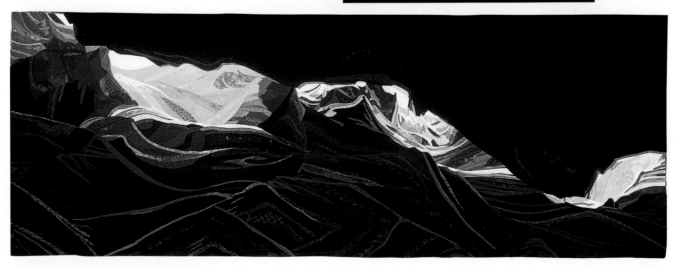

Antelope Canyon, 96" x 36", 1999. Collection of Larry and Sheryl Pasquini.

The canyons are very skinny, deep cuts in the earth made from flash floods flowing through the sandstone. Our guide loved these canyons and knew everything about them. He knew the best spots to photograph. He often told us, "If you'll just squat down back in that hollow and hold your head to the side like so, and look up on that wall you will see the image of a bear," or shark, or some such animal. Then he shared a Native American folk tale about that part of the canyon.

The color at the rim where the sun hits can be yellow, bright orange, or red and, as you look down the wall farther from the light, you see incredible blues and purples.

Three photographs were put together to create a long rectangular composition. The colors were so fabulous in the photograph that I did not use a painting but followed the colors, adding three circles as ghosts.

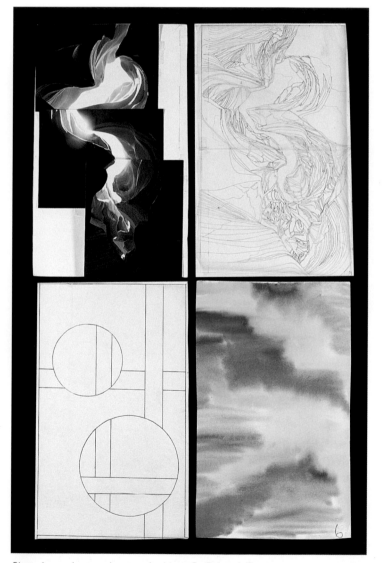

Photo, base, ghost, and watercolor layers for Painted Canyon.

I was asked to teach in Flagstaff, Arizona, at "Quilt Camp in the Pines" in July. It is a wonderful conference and my suite-mate was to be Yvonne Porcella. I had seen the slot canyons in January; what would it be like to go back when the sun would be directly overhead? I called Darcy Falk, a fiber artist who lives in Flagstaff, and Yvonne and I met her at the airport and drove four hours north to the canyons.

We decided to go into the Lower Canyons since I had already been in the Upper Antelope Canyons. The guide said it wasn't too hard—there weren't too many big rocks to climb over or too many stairs to climb. I don't know about that—maybe I am getting old, but there were a lot of rocks and a lot of stairs—but the canyon was spectacular! The lower canyons are not as deep, so there was more light at the bottom. It would be hard to tell which canyon I liked better; they were both so different.

Three photographs were put together to make the composition; the ghost is two circles intersected by long rectangles. The painting was done so the colors blend together and follow the contours of the canyon.

Painted Canyon, 54" x 90",
2000. Collection of Ardis and
Robert James, given to the
International Quilt Study Center
in honor of Professor Craig.
Used with permission of the
International Quilt Study Center
at the University of Nebraska.

Glass Carafes

Glass Carafes, 39" x 57", 1999.

Every Wednesday night that I am in town my friend Sherry and I play cards, usually cribbage. I kept talking about wanting to do a still-life quilt. Sherry has some of the most beautiful glass carafes, one of which my husband and I brought back for her from Germany (the tall one in the middle). She suggested I bring my camera and we would see what we could do. So, the following Wednesday, we set up some boxes on the table and draped them with black cloth. I had my camera on a tripod and used a cheap floodlight. Sherry moved the floodlight around to change the shadows and reflections while I clicked away.

The ghost is the stopper of the round bottle enlarged and placed in the center and upper-right corner. These circles add to the illusion of glass. No painting was used.

For *Glass Carafes with Checks*, Sherry and I set up a checkerboard cloth and took another roll of film. The reflections of the checks in the stoppers of the carafes were really enticing.

The painting consists of three colors blending into each other. The ghost is a larger version of the check.

Glass Carafes with Checks, 30" x 36 1/2", 1999.

Hawaii Quilts

Leaves *(Varagate heliconia)*, 19½" x 29", 1999.

I was asked to teach at the Hawaii Quilt Conference held on Kauai in 1999, and was invited to bring someone. My husband doesn't care for the sun and the beach, so I asked my friend Randi if she would accompany me. It's a tough job, but someone has to do it! We had a marvelous time. I taught for the first week; each night after class we went exploring. After the conference, we stayed for another week in a bungalow in a little town. It was like we actually lived there. We did a lot of hiking, diving, and shopping. I took the next set of pictures during a guided tour of the botanical gardens.

Two photographs of the same leaves but from different angles were superimposed to create this abstract. One is the base and the second is the ghost. Brighter colors than the actual leaves are used.

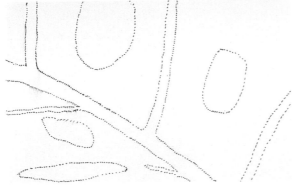

Photo of the philodendron leaf and the ghost drawing.

The gardens and lush foliage of Hawaii are overwhelming. We took many self-guided walking tours through the jungle in the rain and sun. We once ended up on the cliff overlooking the Na Pali coast.

When looking at the beach below, it seemed we should be able to touch the wings of the birds soaring overhead. The sheer drop was long and incredible, the view was expansive, serene, and breathtakingly beautiful. Soul-filling!

The colors were so great in this photograph that I did not do a painting. The ghost is a close-up of the upper-left corner of the philodendron, blown up as if you were looking through a large leaf at the two philodendrons.

Split Leaf Philodendron (Swiss cheese monstera), 34¹/₂" x 23¹/₂", 1999.

The last day of our stay we took a helicopter ride with Chuck from Air Kauai. We recommend a ride with Chuck if you ever are in Kauai; he has the most incredible music collection and would change the music as we flew over the coffee fields, through the rain forest, and alongside a volcano with all of the waterfalls. We then flew around the Na Pali coast and saw the edge we had stood on the previous day! A snowy white owl flew by us, and Chuck said that in the eighteen years he had been touring, he had rarely seen this happen. It was a special day!

Palms, 51 1/2" x 34", 1999. Collection of Jackie Evans.

We flew home via Honolulu. During a four-hour layover, Randi went to visit some friends, and I went to the botanical gardens in Honolulu. What I noticed most was the size of the plants—everything was huge! I wandered around the gardens for several hours, watching the colors change in the leaves and listening to the birds.

Again, the colors were so great in the photograph that I did not use a painting. The exciting part of the photo is where the fronds overlap to create the great woven graphic of shadows and light; that section was enlarged to use as the ghost.

We swam with the turtles! We went to the end of Ke`e Beach to watch the sunset. We noticed there were a lot of people snorkeling and, as they came up the beach, they were very animated. There were hundreds of turtles feeding on the reef! We had no bathing suits, snorkels, or fins! The turtle is my totem; I *had* to swim with the turtles. Were we brave enough to borrow some gear and swim in our underwear? NO! So the next day, our last, we rented our own equipment and donned our bathing suits. I actually held hand to flipper with this majestic guy. I would say this was one of the best experiences of my life. I made this little quilt to thank Randi for swimming with me (she's terrified of the ocean!).

Old Man Turtle, 24" square, 1999. Collection of Randi Perkins.

New Studio Quilts

March 24, 2000 was a great day It was my tenth wedding anniversary and we celebrated it by moving into our new house. We had been living in a one-bedroom guesthouse on our property for nine years as we waited to build our dream house.

Several weeks after moving day my beautiful studio was all set up, and I was dying to work on a quilt. I had no inspiration in my photo album, and no time to go on a journey away from home to find one. I took a walk through the old part of Santa Fe and photographed the little side streets filled with adobe buildings. It was a great way to discover the uniqueness of Santa Fe's buildings. The photos taken that day inspired these next three quilts.

Colored Village uses a mind painting and perspective bricks as the ghost. I used the brightest colors I could find.

Colored Village, *36" square, 2000.*

As you have probably already guessed, I love to do black and white quilts. This little quilt has circles that spin out from the center, appearing to magnify sections of the building.

Black and White Village, *36" square, 2000.*

This third quilt in the series is a combination of the previous two. Three colors of paint were used: a big yellow square, a red rectangle, and an orange corner shape. The rest of the quilt was done in black and whites. The ghosts are one large circle that is lighter and six small circles that are darker.

Painted Village, *36" x 40", 2000.*

Student Works

The following quilts are works from students who completed at least one sample and then went on to create their own masterpiece. It is very exciting to see this process work for so many different ideas.

Ghost Experiment
Ann P. Shaw
Oakton, VA
26" x 42", 1999.

In this piece I experimented with cutting apart the background grid to create an irregular border. The "ghosts" were created from the superimposed background pieces and some additional stripes. The blue and yellow color washes were also superimposed to create green.

Whirligig

Jacquelyn Nouveau, Chapel Hill, NC

35¹/₂" x 54", 1999.

Photo by Seth Tice-Lewis.

Window with a View

Nancy Wasserman, Winchester, MA

35" x 46", 2000.

Photo by artist.

View *was inspired by a photograph of the old walled city of Dubrovnik, Yugoslavia. Because of past war, the city may not exist today.*

Pear Abstraction

Jacquelyn Nouveau, Chapell Hill, NC

33¹/₂" x 44¹/₂", 1999.

Photo by Seth Tice-Lewis.

This quilt and Whirligig, page 66, were explorations in taking a complicated detail and integrating it back into the overall quilt scheme. I think this process introduced more energy and interest.

Cosmic Calypso

Diane Harris, Miami, FL

24" square, 1999.

Ode to Flying Spinnaker, *Vivian Mahlab, Austin, TX, 32" x 38¹/2", 2000.*

With Katie's techniques, I am now able to capture movement and light in my quilts, which was something that had been difficult for me to express through quilting. The quilt was inspired by a photograph by Stanley Rosenfeld entitled "Flying Spinnakers" ©Rosenfeld Collection at the Museum of America and the Sea, Mystic, CT.

Agave
Ann Gail Peterson, Davis, CA
48³/4" x 33", 2000.

Agave *is based on close-up photos taken of an agave (a large succulent) along a rural road outside of Davis, CA. I chose to use a subtle color wash of blue and green over the teal of the leaves and emphasized the black spines along the sides and tip by using Ultrasuede. Much of the quilting was done from the back following the pattern of the fabric; satin stitching was done from the front following the shape of the leaves. The ghosts are two large leaf shapes.*

Ulu
Debbie Nakamora, Kapaa, HI,
30" square, 1999.
Photo by artist.

Dunes

Andrea Limmer, Arlington, VA

24" x 19", 2000.

The background is my favorite place—the beach—with sand dunes, beach grass, and a storm fence. The circles of my ghost layer represent the sun and the spots you see when you close your eyes in the hot sun. The rectangle ghosts repeat the fence posts as a form of shadows. The red and yellow color washes are the patterns made by heat and sun.

Spring Zephyr

Marjorie A. DeQuincy, Sacramento, CA

32" x 42", 2000.

Spring Zephyr uses the color-washed ghost to move the viewer through the medium, light, and dark values in the garden. Katie's techniques add visual excitement to the piece.

Grand Canyon No. 1

Robert S. Leathers, Ithaca, NY

42" x 28", 2000.

Photo by artist.

The inspiration for the quilt above came from sketches I did of the Grand Canyon, and from a petroglyph found in Monument Valley. The ghost landscape approach was particularly appropriate for capturing the mystical illusion of haunted canyons.

Fascinatin' Rhythms
Phyllis Cullen
52" x 73", 2000.
Machine pieced, appliquéd, and quilted.

Jazz is multilayered music, composed of individual innovation and the influence of every musician who has played before. This was the source for the ghostly quartet—the piano, horn, sax, and bass players. The color changes are notes—the color of the music.

A Visit to My Studio

I have a new studio! After nine years of living in a little guest house with an admittedly large studio (but the ceiling was only six feet high!), I finally have a huge studio with a ten foot ceiling. It has four skylights, so on most days I don't even turn the lights on. I have a wonderful view of my favorite plateau.

Views of Katie's fabulous new quilting space.

I have all my favorite things around me:

- A huge 4' x 8' table in the center of the room covered with a rotary cutting mat

- A Horn of America table allows me to quilt forever without my wrists hurting

- My Pfaff® sewing machine

- A huge wall (10 feet tall!) to which I can pin my work-in-progress

- A three-section thread rack to hold all of my Gutermann threads

- A large storage closet to hide all of my stuff and my Hobbs Wool Batting

- My wire drawers to hold all of my fabrics

- Good speakers for my music.

I'm in heaven!

About the Author

Fiber Artist Katie Pasquini Masopust has traveled the United States, Canada, New Zealand, Australia, Japan, Belgium, Switzerland, and England teaching contemporary quilt design. She has changed her style over the years, starting with traditional works, then creating mandalas, followed by dimensional quilts. She enjoys landscapes, and feels as if she has returned full circle to her beginning as a painter; now she paints with fabric.

Several of Katie's quilts have been featured in *Quilter's Newsletter Magazine* and she was included in *Fiber Arts* magazine (July/August 1983) in the "Gallery." Her first one-woman show in Eureka, California was the catalyst for a teaching career. Her most recent one-woman show was held at the Shidoni Gallery in Tesuque, New Mexico.

Kiru Shiru was featured on the cover of *American Quilter* in April 1987, and an article on Katie's designs using isometric perspective appeared in the April 1991 issue. *American Quilter* again featured Katie's work as a cover story on *Fractured Landscapes* in the spring of 1995, and an article on her new work, "Ghost Layers and Color Washes" appeared in the Summer 1999 issue.

Katie is also the author of *Mandala: For contemporary quilt designs and other medium*, and *The Contemporary Sampler*, both reprinted by Dover, and *Three-Dimensional Design*, *Isometric Perspective*, and *Fractured Landscapes*, all published by C&T Publishing.

Katie has won many awards throughout her career, including Best of Show at the Houston Quilt Festival in 1982 and 1986, at the Pacific International Quilt Show 1994, and First and Second at the AQS show 1995. Her piece *Dimensional Portal* was in the 1991 Quilt National and won the People's Choice award. Recently, *Passages, Chaco Canyon* won the Penny Nii award at the 1998 Visions show, and her quilt *Rio Hondo* was chosen as one of the 100 quilts of the twentieth century.

Subject Index

Quilt Index

KATIE'S MASTERPIECES

STUDENT MASTERPIECES

Page Gettman

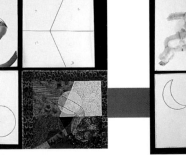

Christa Manning

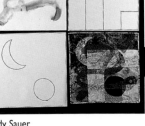

Judy Sauer

Clouds, 54" x 42", 2000. Collection of Trish Kogan.

Other Fine Books From C&T Publishing

Along the Garden Path: More Quilters and Their Gardens, Jean Wells and Valorie Wells

The Art of Machine Piecing: Quality Workmanship Through a Colorful Journey, Sally Collins

Block Magic: Over 50 Fun & Easy Blocks made from Squares and Rectangles, Nancy Johnson-Srebro

Civil War Women: Their Quilts, Their Roles, and Activities for Re-Enactors, Barbara Brackman

Color Play: Easy Steps to Imaginative Color in Quilts, Joen Wolfrom

Cotton Candy Quilts: Using Feed Sacks, Vintage and Reproduction Fabrics, Mary Mashuta

Cut-Loose Quilts: Stack, Slice, Switch & Sew, Jan Mullen

Fantastic Fabric Folding: Innovative Quilting Projects, Rebecca Wat

Floral Stitches: An Illustrated Guide, Judith Baker Montano

Flower Pounding: Quilt Projects for All Ages, Amy Sandrin & Ann Frischkorn

Hand Appliqué with Alex Anderson: Seven Projects for Hand Appliqué, Alex Anderson

In the Nursery: Creative Quilts and Designer Touches, Jennifer Sampou & Carolyn Schmitz

Quilting with the Muppets: The Jim Henson Company in Association with Sesame Workshop

Setting Solutions, Sharyn Craig

Shadow Redwork with Alex Anderson: 24 Designs to Mix and Match, Alex Anderson

Snowflakes & Quilts, Paula Nadelstern

For quilting supplies:
Cotton Patch Mail Order
3405 Hall Lane, Dept. CTB
Lafayette, CA 94549
(800) 835-4418
(925) 283-7883
e-mail: quiltusa@yahoo.com
website: www.quiltusa.com

Marjorie A. DeQuincy

For more information write for a free catalog:

C&T Publishing, Inc., P.O. Box 1456, Lafayette, CA 94549
(800) 284-1114, e-mail: ctinfo@ctpub.com, website: www.ctpub.com